Part I
Exporting Silicon Valley

CHAPTER 1

How Silicon Valley Thinks: The Quest to be KING

Silicon Valley has an amazing secret.

When you live outside of Silicon Valley—perhaps somewhere in the United States, or maybe Mexico, or anywhere in the world—all a person sees from the outside looking in is the great business success of the area.

When people visit Silicon Valley, the California home of many of the most successful technology companies in the world, they expect to find a place where the streets are filled with venture capitalists and entrepreneurs continually thinking about how to create the next great company. And they do.

From the coffee shops to the university dorm rooms, it becomes readily apparent why this area is the leading hub for the high-tech sector, accounting for one-third of all venture capital investment in the United States. What is not so apparent is how the good things that happen in Silicon Valley really happen. That is a secret worth discovering.

The term Silicon Valley originally referred to the region's large number of silicon chip innovators and manufacturers, but eventually came to refer to all the technology businesses in the area. Located about 45 miles southeast of San Francisco, Silicon Valley is situated in Santa Clara County, California. The area is approximately 25 miles long and 10 miles wide, sandwiched between San Francisco Bay and the hills of San Jose.

My Connection to Silicon Valley

Seven years ago I came to Silicon Valley from Mexico to help train executives from my homeland on how to do business in Silicon Valley and the United States. I used to think starting a company was very easy. You get an idea, you talk to some people to determine the need, and you start building a great product. But Silicon Valley gave me a wonderful gift: a new mindset.

My discovery was that the mindset of Silicon Valley is to think beyond the start-up phase. In the minds of the Silicon Valley company creators, it is not enough to merely have a great product and to do well in your neighborhood. Company creators must think beyond their local boundaries. The question to ask is: how do we grow regionally, nationally, or even internationally?

This mindset is a simple concept but not an easy process. In fact, this can be a huge mental challenge for many company leaders in other lands. The first time that they go to the next biggest city near their town, they might discover that the things that worked great in their own town do not necessarily work the same way outside their hometown.

This is especially true with service oriented companies. Perhaps they find a local need, start to solve it and then are pleased with their success in their own neighborhood. The company leaders are proud they are able to deliver a service that is in demand. But then they might venture out from their own neighborhood. Now as they travel to other places they discover that the competition is quite strong, and there are other companies doing the same kinds of services they provide. The competition has a high degree of competence, and being able to successfully expand becomes a complex problem to solve.

However, there exists a proven way to make those jumps smoothly and successfully. Helping companies make those leaps by thinking like Silicon Valley thinks is the work that I have chosen. That is the reason I have written this book. Personally I have helped more than 400 companies from outside the United States come to Silicon Valley and discover that the way of doing business here is quite different. True, all companies are unique, but the key is to discover how the Silicon Valley companies are alike.

A Brief History of Silicon Valley

The history of Silicon Valley is the story of two extraordinary research universities and some companies that started in ordinary garages.

Since it was founded in 1891, Stanford University in Palo Alto, California, was dedicated to the mission of serving the regional interests of the American west. Stanford University students were encouraged to start their own companies rather than go to the east and join the "establishment."

Stanford University was founded as an alternative to a nearby great college, the giant University of California at Berkeley, founded in 1868. Over the years UC Berkeley has had 47 faculty members and alumni win the Nobel Prize. The small but mighty Stanford faculty and alumni have received 26 Nobel Prizes.

The region around Stanford became home to an electronics industry, which began through experimentation and innovation in the fields of radio, television, and military electronics. Obviously Stanford and its graduates played a major role in the development of this area.

In 1939 two Stanford engineering graduate students set out to create their own company in a garage in Palo Alto. That company went on to become HP (Hewlett-Packard), a company that became a global electronics giant.

After World War II a Stanford professor of electrical engineering, Frederick Terman, conceived of an idea to establish the Stanford Industrial Park by leasing part of the university's land to high-tech companies for 99 years. Like a catalyst in chemistry, the industrial park sparked a "Big Bang" like chain of events, sparking a string of technology revolutions.

What followed from the 1950s to the 1970s was a series of inventions, all made from "silicon," including the first microprocessor chip at Intel in 1971, which launched the computer revolution.

By then, several big companies such as General Electric, Ford Philco, and IBM established their facilities in Palo Alto and other neighboring cities such as Mountain View and San Jose. The phrase Silicon Valley was coined by journalist Don C. Hoefler in 1971 in a series of articles for *Electronic News*, a weekly industry trade publication.

The personal computer revolution began in Silicon Valley when Apple was founded in 1976 by Steve Jobs and UC Berkeley grad, Steve Wozniak. Apple's first computer was manufactured in the Jobs family's garage. Innovation and garage lore continued.

In 1998 Stanford Ph.D. students Larry Page and Sergey Brin started a business from a garage in the San Jose suburb of Menlo Park, California. The search engine company they created, Google, became a leader in the World Wide Web revolution (which naturally also had its origins in Silicon Valley back in 1969).

Innovation Tourism

Hundreds of people have called me from universities, companies, and business associations from around the globe to ask if they could visit our offices in Silicon Valley. They request us to arrange meetings with companies like Apple, HP, Yahoo, and on and on. The draw to be an innovation tourist is obviously amazing.

Recently a company owner came to me and said, "Hey, I want to visit Google because if I can get inside there I should be able to create a great company."

"Well, I have some friends we can call," I said, "but I don't see how you think that just by visiting a place will be good enough to discover all the secrets of having a great company."

When I called my contact at Google and requested the tour, he naturally asked why we wanted the meeting.

"A good friend of mine thinks that touring your offices will be enough for him to discover how to create a great company like Google," I said.

Together we laughed and laughed. But the person from Google agreed to give us a tour of the places where visitors are allowed and then have dinner together. "I will be very curious to ask after walking around the Google campus how the magic of one great company can help create another great and different company," he said.

We enjoyed the visit to Google and the great dinner conversation that followed. My out-of-town entrepreneur friend is a smart, visionary and funny guy. We discussed many topics about business and our careers, and then the conversation turned to the subject of the tour.

"What magic did you discover that is going to trigger your capability to create a great innovative company?" asked the man from Google.

My friend had to admit that when we walked around Google it basically looked like any other software company in the world. There were cubicles, computer screens, conference rooms with whiteboards, and places to get coffee. The restrooms posted challenging questions on the walls and the employee lounge has a great pool table, but other than that, it was the same.

My friend discovered that a tourist visit is not enough. At dinner we began to discuss the hidden aspects that make a Silicon Valley company like Google great. To unlock the mystery, some study is required. But that is the good news. If it were easy, then every company would be doing it.

However, for those willing to search for the clues, a reward worth a king's ransom awaits.

Thinking Like a KING

To discover the real magic, you have to begin with the question: What do Silicon Valley companies have in common? An interesting book by economist Tapan Munroe, *What Makes Silicon Valley Tick?*, examined the key elements of the valley's long-standing prosperity. Munroe says Silicon Valley's economy is unique, but there are lessons to be learned.

A first lesson is these companies don't look different. But the thinking is different.

Listen carefully to the exchanges at the association meetings and brainstorming sessions over morning coffee in Palo Alto and Menlo Park. Eavesdrop on some lunch discussions throughout the cafes and sandwich shops from San Francisco to San Jose. As you walk across the campuses of Stanford and UC Berkeley, listen to the thoughtful conversations of the students sitting on the lawns or taking study breaks in the student union. At each location you can hear Silicon Valley people thinking aloud about their aspirations to create the next great idea that will be tested on the market. They hope to be the people who "think up" the next technology revolution.

Silicon Valley is unique and cannot be replicated, although many communities in America and other parts of the world have tried. This is a unique ecosystem that grew organically and cannot be artificially recreated. What can be replicated is the thinking approach to creating a company.

Here is an easy way to remember the mindset. You can't spell the word "thinking" without the letters K I N G. In the minds of the Silicon Valley company creators, there is a quest to create a company that I label by the acronym K I N G. Each letter explains a key element of how Silicon Valley is thinking:

K stands for Knowledge. These are companies that leverage knowledge, the kinds of knowledge that can be easily and cheaply mined through computers.

I stands for Innovation. Silicon Valley brains are driven by the need to innovate, perhaps the only way to sustain prosperity.

N stands for National. The mantra of Silicon Valley is to grow, and the growth means looking beyond the local region to a broader national market.

G stands for Global. Growing nationally is never good enough. Growing beyond national borders is the real prize.

All these four aspects are quite interesting to understand. Great companies come out of the Silicon Valley because of a combination of intelligence, resources, experience, and openness to create KING companies.

What Can You Do Abroad?

Silicon Valley insiders have known for a long time that this region is really an entire ecosystem that is spawning these KING companies. Entrepreneurs see a problem or need. Inventors create technology to solve those needs. Investors come to the table and provide more than financial resources, but also insights on how to create a KING company.

If you cannot replicate the Silicon Valley, what is left for the people that live abroad?

Many of my friends are disappointed when they come to understand the uniqueness of Silicon Valley. But the good news is you can understand what a Silicon Valley company thinks about and how that mindset can be exported to your own town.

Begin by brainstorming the problems that you have in your own town. How could knowledge be leveraged to solve those problems? What could you do to innovate to solve the problem? Is this a problem that other towns in your country also face? Is this a problem that towns in other nations also must deal with?

The following pages explain how to take the answers to those questions and use a proven process to create or transform a company. This is a process that employs the thinking of Silicon Valley with a practical step by step approach. As you take these steps, I will guide you along each part of the journey. With that thinking in mind, we are ready to start your quest to be a KING like Silicon Valley.

CHAPTER 2

How to Think in Silicon Valley (Without Losing Your Local Mindset)

Silicon Valley is a place where people are always thinking about how to make the next move. They are always probing how to innovate with the next technology and dreaming up how to create a product or service that is going to be of use around the world. In this way, Silicon Valley is not so much a place as it is a mindset.

Don't get me wrong—visiting Silicon Valley is a great experience. Once I had a call from a representative from

China when he had just arrived at an event at Stanford University. The man said it was his first time visiting Silicon Valley and he wanted me to explain to him the exact boundaries of Silicon Valley.

That is a very complex question. Why? Because Silicon Valley is not a specific place where innovation happens. I told him that Silicon Valley is a huge space that runs from San Francisco to Santa Clara and is home to hundreds of thousands of companies, from very small startups to huge corporations.

What unites the area is not geography, I explained to him, but a way of thinking. This mindset stems from the great universities, associations, venture capital firms, start-ups, and corporations. Silicon Valley, in fact, is everything that is here.

People talk about creating a "Silicon Valley" in another place, but I think this is impossible. Silicon Valley is really greater than the sum of its parts. The synergy from the combination of characteristics can never be duplicated.

The Characteristics of Silicon Valley

One of the best characteristics of Silicon Valley that I have found is **openness**. In certain industries, people may believe their ideas need to be kept secret until they are ready to launch in that particular market. In the Silicon Valley, it can be quite different.

People are willing to discuss ideas: how a little adjustment may revolutionize social media; how something else can change music devices; how providing medicine to people could be done in a new way. By speaking openly about an idea you can get crucial feedback and recommendations from outside sources that can help you take it further.

To this end, it is vital that you be strong in networking. In Silicon Valley, there are events everywhere. Organizations such as TiE Global (www.tie.org) started there with a small group of professionals and now hold events around the world for those interested in entrepreneurship. Similar groups organize hundreds of events each year.

This type of event can also show you another of Silicon Valley's best characteristics: **thinking big**. Remember though, that thinking big doesn't mean that you are going to start big. Thinking big is about having a vision of where your company is headed in the next five years and beyond. Once you have the big end result, you can start reverse engineering the steps to get there.

What many people notice when they meet with people in the Silicon Valley is their **curiosity** and desire to learn from those they encounter. The companies there have people from different countries and different backgrounds, all working together and sharing their different ideas. If you visit from abroad and attend a networking event, people will be eager to learn about the mindsets in your country and local environment. This curious nature can be a huge strength because incorporating different points of view can help generate great ideas.

Along the same lines, working with other people can produce excellent results. Sure, you have a big idea and the vision of what your company will be; but you will never be able to realize it on your own. **Think collaboratively**—what are the complementary skills that you don't have? If you are a great programmer you need somebody that can create and manage a great business model. If you are good at marketing your ideas, you need to have operational people that can build the company.

Part of thinking big is that you want to create wealth, not just for yourself, but for the company as a whole. If you generate value that can be shared among the participants, they will be invested in the success. Many, however, would like to have their company be completely their own. If you want 100% ownership, ask yourself, do you have 100% of the resources to build the company? If you don't have all the skills required to perform all the tasks needed, then as you assemble your company, **wealth sharing will be as important as wealth creation.**

Another essential characteristic of Silicon Valley is that they really believe in the concept that **failure is a vital learning experience**. You will experiment with prototypes and concepts, but you need to be prepared that your initial idea will not work out. "Fail fast" is a phrase I love because failure allows you to learn. If your idea doesn't work, go to your collaborators and others that you share ideas with. These people will look at your failure and give you feedback about why your idea has not been working, perhaps something you may not have even considered.

The failure and subsequent feedback allows you to figure out how you need to twist your idea. Maybe it needs to be exposed or marketed in a different way. Perhaps the market you are addressing is not the right market. Or there is a better technology that you could use to achieve your result. Maybe you are going through the wrong channel and you should try a different model for distributing the product. This process can help to solve issues you knew about and, more importantly, those you did not.

Failing fast is an incredibly powerful concept. In the Silicon Valley, when the people fail they don't feel bad; they feel they got valuable experience. They realize that they learned vital information and are able to come back with a new idea, a new approach, a new opportunity.

Seeing failure as an opportunity can be hard to wrap your head around. In many business cultures, people may want to distance themselves from their failures. But in the Silicon Valley, it is the opposite. A brilliant example of this idea in action is the FailCon, which describes itself as a one-day conference for technology entrepreneurs, investors, developers, and designers to study their own and others' failures and prepare for success. Since 2009, hundreds have come together to constructively discuss failures and learn from the business mistakes of others. Nowhere else in the world will you find such pride in failure.

There is an interesting book called *On Competition* by Michael E. Porter of the Harvard Business School, which addresses another great characteristic of Silicon Valley: your **competition is a valuable resource**. How can you see the competition as a resource? When you have an idea and start to do your due diligence, you will find that there are several that are trying to solve the same problem. You have two ways to go: avoid them to protect your idea or work with them.

Any real problem will have many people working to solve it. Talking to the competitors can allow you to learn from each other so that you are all able to move forward faster. Of course, it is always going to be a bit of a race and proprietary knowledge still needs to be protected. But you need to realize that, at times, the knowledge that you are getting is of greater value than the risk of exposing your idea. You may need to learn how to discuss your work without revealing too much. You don't show the core of your idea in a way that you are just giving your competition the magic sauce.

At the same time, you can't spend too much time being worried about the competition stealing your idea. Yes, the idea is there, but it doesn't have value until there is execution or knowledge of how to build a solution and a plan for how that solution is coming into the market. All those things are the real value and the "trick" of how successful startups really grow to be big is because they know how to learn together with competing businesses. At times, you may find out that your competition has a half of the idea solved and you have the other side. Perhaps you can get together and create something successful, instead of worrying and fighting to find some resources that they already have.

Innovation is a key to many industries and we need to understand innovation as not only how to solve problems in a new way, but also new ways to go about creating those solutions. Sometimes innovation is understood as the big change in technology. But innovation in Silicon Valley can mean radically changing how things are done at any stage, any level, and in any area of your business. That is why the value of innovation comes into your capital. Remember that sometimes very simple things are very, very important for solving the problem.

People in their role of creating value, as entrepreneurs or as part of companies, require experimentation to test ideas, using different methods that run from scientific approaches to a very informal set of activities. The testing idea can be from a whole new concept related to overall innovation or just a small part on the side of business, manufacturing, or distribution. I was really surprised to learn how vital to the culture of the Silicon Valley the concept of testing and validating ideas can be. This will be covered in Chapter 7, but briefly, this approach of testing ideas is often known as Innovation Labs, where the people build an idea, create a value proposition, and throughout experimentation validate the market traction and the business model viability.

Another important characteristic is **thinking globally**. If you want to truly innovate, sometimes you must look further than the competition next door. The same problem could have a very different solution in Finland than you might find in Brazil. Not only is it essential to study global businesses, but to integrate people from a variety of cultures into your team.

In my organization, TechBA, we do a huge amount of work with Mexican companies. Recently, we have been helping our Mexican clients incorporate people from all around the world into their business. Human resources are so critical to building a successful business and bringing together people from a variety of places can be valuable. And if you remember what I said about sharing the wealth, these employees will be truly invested in helping to build the company.

Another characteristic that may seem strange is that, in the Silicon Valley, **your company is always for sale.** In a lot of countries, creating a company is very personal and you may expect that company will hold your name forever and be an inheritance for your children. But here in the Silicon Valley, the company is all part of the product that you want to sell. At any stage you should be willing to sell.

You come up with an idea, convert that idea into a product, and then that product starts to be on the market. But if you don't have the resources to scale the company, one of the things you do is try to figure out who wants to integrate your technology into some other property. When you have a company that is already on the market and you need a huge amount of resources to get the product out to the consumer, you may consider that this can be an opportunity to sell your company to some large organization that has already reached to the specific market you want to get.

The mindset of "my company is for sale" is very, very important. Of course, not all companies will be sold. Perhaps you are going to be the leader in your market, but that happens for very few companies. Usually, 7% of the companies that get angel investments reach a good exit[1]. Most are medium-sized companies that are not really going to be the best or the biggest company in the world.

Another way to understand the concept of "always for sale" is in the sense that you may want to grow, and you will do it by getting investment into your company with the desire to bring your company into an IPO. In this situation you are selling a piece of your company in exchange of a venture capital investment. This includes your investors as part of your IPO strategy, which is a very different approach from simply selling your company.

In the Silicon Valley, they **work hard**. They do whatever it is needed to make things happen—that means working long hours, working on weekends, and making sure that all employees know that everybody shares the responsibility for moving the company forward.

As the saying goes, "Time is money." This can sometimes be hard for other cultures to understand, particularly those from Latin America. In the Silicon Valley, you get into

---

[1] *Fool's Gold?: The Truth Behind Angel Investing In America,* Scott A. Shane, 2008.

a meeting and you need to keep the discussion right to the point. Don't spend too much time making small talk; get down to why you came there, the subject or idea you need to talk about, what you want to build, and what specific resources or feedback you need from them. Silicon Valley is hugely productive, because the people are really focusing on how to do things well and quickly. Even though "time is money," they are not focused on the money. The most important thing is to build something great and that will generate the money in the end.

Many believe that the Silicon Valley is the greatest place in the world for developing technologies. This is true but it misses part of the picture. Yes, there are unique universities and fantastic research labs that are there, all working to create something brand new. But in order to be valuable, technology needs to have a way to reach the market. This element cannot be overlooked and I try to emphasize it to the companies that I work with.

Marketing and technology adoption go hand in hand and they must be considered together as part of your overall idea. On top of the marketing and technology it is an additional element that integrates other activities under the hood of business development. Within the Silicon Valley, people know how to get **technology out to those that will use it** and this is an extremely valuable skill. That is why it isn't just electronics, but biotech, alternative energies, and other types of technologies that are making their way to the market from the Silicon Valley.

Those that work in Silicon Valley are **constantly innovating**. This may be one of the most important characteristics that you can learn from. I don't just mean this in terms of creating new technologies either; the people of Silicon

Valley are always looking for a new method or collaboration that can help at any stage of the business.

How Silicon Valley Characteristics Can Translate to Any Company

I came to the Silicon Valley to understand how they create successful companies in order to help translate the process for companies anywhere. I identified three very valuable elements in their process: vision, value chain, and position.

Vision. Creating a unique vision will help guide you as you build your company. Mentors are a great source of knowledge to build that vision. Talk with people that have already done great things in the same field, with a similar type of solution or even those that took a quite different approach. From these discussions, form a plan for where you want to head.

Value Chain. An important point that I found in the Silicon Valley is, you usually don't want to build a startup that is trying to do everything for everyone. A typical mistake that I found is that companies want to build an enterprise resource program so they can manage the resources and administrative systems. But if you talk to people here, they are looking how to build a specific tool; not a value chain of the entire company at once. Find what you can build that serves a specific need and that allows you to grow in an unattended market. Your startup has very limited resources; you need to find how to use them in the best way. If you figure out how to do that and focus into various small areas, you are going to be more successful.

Position. When you want to build a full ERP or the full product, often you start to see the big problems. You may find it is going to take forever or it is going to take a lot of resources, or there is already major competition. When you focus into a very narrow area of market opportunity, you have the biggest chance to be successful. Your specific area of opportunity is your position. You may find it requires an alliance to some big company or supplier. You may have a unique idea that is for a niche market and collaboration with an already successful company would allow you to focus on it.

Your own local point of view may be very different from some of the things I've talked about so far. The Latin American people for instance, want to build the relationship first, and then we build the business. The idea of a company that is merchandise that you can sell goes against how most people create companies there.

Also, resources vary from place to place. This can be the human resources of your team or funding opportunities or access to equipment. Resources are almost always scarcer than you'd like, but you need to figure out how to use the resources that you have on hand and use them well. Look at your environment and see what things in your market can be used in some other places in the world. A simplistic example is food; many dishes that are popular in one place may be hard to find in another. Can you imagine eating *chile relleno* in China? But people import foreign cuisines to new places all the time and often give it their own spin. What from your environment can you bring into the other places in the world?

Your local resources can be very powerful when you use them in a new way. How you bring innovation from different points of view and put it all together to solve problems is crucial. Put things into your own context with creativity and see the difference. This is the key to learning from the mindset of the Silicon Valley. During this book, we are going to be talking about how to apply these lessons from Silicon Valley to create the greatest and most fantastic company that you can imagine.

Product Box	Prune The Tree	Buy A Feature
		Remember the Future

Part II
Creating the Silicon Valley Type Company

CHAPTER 3

Finding Innovation Spaces: Begin With Good Networking

In the cultural environment of the Silicon Valley, there is a big association between networking and the creation of new ideas. Naturally, when you gather together smart and creative individuals, innovation happens.

Let's think about how ideas come to life. If you want to find problems that need solving, you can find that by talking to people, reading magazines, and searching in websites. Knowing a problem is one thing, but before you can really start to provide some solutions you must analyze and dissect the issue.

As I said in the last chapter, one of the Silicon Valley's greatest characteristics is the people who are very much open to share ideas. An idea is really of limited value without a plan to bring it to life. Often, discussing your idea with other people can help it to grow and take shape into something with real potential. Those ideas eventually become a solution and that solution becomes a product. That product becomes part of a company; that company becomes part of a business; and that business starts to generate revenues. It is a huge process that requires the work of many people along the way.

So who are these people you might be networking with? Let's discuss the taxonomy of the Silicon Valley networking environment. Sure, you get many of the same categories as anywhere else, but the Silicon Valley has some unique classifications. My nickname for this networking DNA is the triple helix of industry, academia, and government.

Industry: Big Business and Tiny Startups in the Silicon Valley

There are many large companies that are based in the Silicon Valley, many of which were founded there. Google, HP, Symantec, Yahoo, Intel, Apple—the list goes on and on. This is a huge ecosystem and within it are the people that understand all the parts of the business process. The employees at those companies are used to coming up with new ideas to solve the really big problems. They know their market; they know the logistics to put out their products; they know how to provide support. This knowledge base can be very valuable as you expand your business.

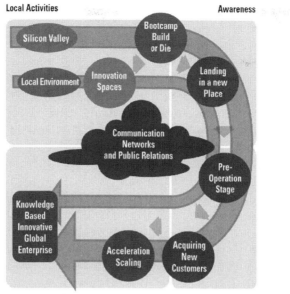

Roadmap to Build a KING company

The other side of the business coin is the startup company. It is said there are more than 25,000 startup companies being built at any one time in the Silicon Valley. These people will have similar experiences in terms of building a business from the ground up. They can understand starting with just a kernel of an idea and working hard to grow it into something substantial.

Academia: University as Innovator

One of the Silicon Valley's greatest assets is the proximity to amazing universities. The academic environment is very powerful and businesses are able to collaborate with such institutions as Stanford University and the University of California, Berkeley. In addition, there are other excellent universities in the California State system and private universities like Santa Clara University nearby.

The academic environment provides two different groups of people that can be valuable to your networking. Of course, the professors are very knowledgeable and have a great background in research and development. But consider also, the students, who are eager to get involved with a company and develop mentorship possibilities.

Universities have become excellent environments for technology innovators. Google, one of the largest and most important technology companies in the world, was started by two Stanford University PhD students.

Government: Behind the Scenes

Although the Silicon Valley doesn't have an obvious strong governmental presence like Washington DC, it is definitely there. Government can support by offering contracts that motivate innovation across industry and academia. People in this field can help point you to sources of funding you may have not considered.

Silicon Valley Networking

When I first came to live in the Silicon Valley in 2005, I was surprised to find that you could go to a networking event every single day of the year. There are professional organizations like TiE Global and SVForum that have regular events to provide innovation spaces where people can gather and share knowledge. That is where you are able to meet people to discuss ideas and to find potential alliances, co-founders, investors, and customers; perhaps you'll even find competitors who want to discuss what is in the marketplace.

Like Eleanor Roosevelt use to say: "Small minds talk about other people; Average minds talk about things; Great minds talk about ideas." That is why the value of Silicon Valley is unique. You are able to get into these networking events and find those "great minds." These are idea people and they are willing to discuss not only their great idea, but also how it was implemented and how they are looking for implementing in the future.

Also, consider the online networking possibilities. It is not an accident that the biggest online social networks are based in the Silicon Valley; the people here understand the values of maintaining connections. Despite that you are able to access them from anywhere in the world, that communication usually started face to face. These online tools are really now to keep that connection—you are still usually searching for specific people that you need to solve a given problem, to find a supplier, to talk to a potential customer, whatever is needed. The online communities that have been created in this area are one of the most valuable resources that you can have to nurture your ideas in this work of innovation and spaces.

Be a Skilled Networker

If you want to talk to these great idea people, you need to develop your networking skills. I don't want to get into how to build your skills, since there is a huge amount of information available online and in books on that topic. But I will mention a couple of interesting points that may help you.

As I've said before, the openness of Silicon Valley is a unique attribute. At networking events you can openly communicate with people from many backgrounds. As you do this, you may notice another quality that seems out of place in a room full of geniuses: humility. They are interested in pushing the boundaries, innovating, and finding new solutions. But they also realize they are not the only person who could do these things. The very fact that they are asking each others opinions shows that they are humble enough to get input from others on how to make their ideas better. Remember this quality as you speak with people about your company.

As you speak to people at events, become a Super Connector. A Super Connector wants to help people find the right person in the room. A great example of a Super Connector is David Cheriton, a Stanford Professor that helped the founders of Google, Larry Page and Sergey Brin, to establish a connection with Andy Bechtolsheim, co-founder of Sun Microsystems, to get the first 100,000 US investments prior to the company creation. Later the connections extended to introduce them to the Venture Capitalist firm Kleiner Perkins Caufield & Byers. Today this is history: Google is a very well know company, David Cheriton is recognized as a billionaire by *Forbes Magazine,* and the impact in our daily life is felt hundreds of times a day.

Keep in mind also, that your "role" may change depending on the type of event you are attending. If you are a very high level technical engineer with the skills in software, maybe you want to listen to talks on how to find venture capital for your company. In that case you are in the "learning role."

But you may also want to take on a "creative role" and promote your own network. For instance, Hacker Dojo is a community where the technical people get together to find out about new software and hardware technologies. That is a great group because the people attending are immersed in this field and generate new ideas together. You could create your own unique group, even starting as small as www.meetup.com, a website that allows you to organize events. This will generate a new circle of interest that could prove a valuable resource for you.

Networking may feel difficult, but the real hard part is to figure out how to invest your time. Time is the most valuable resource that you have and you need to use it wisely. In networking, it is very easy to spend time without making sure the activities will be worthwhile. I find that if you would like to be a good networker, you need to realize that there are important steps before, during and after the event.

Before the event

Before attending a networking event, ask yourself these questions: Why do you want to go to a specific event? What do you expect to get from it? Is it to learn, to teach, to share, to validate, or just to keep up to date in specific areas? If you know what you can bring to the table and you know what you are looking for, that time will be very wisely invested. Otherwise, maybe you are spending too much time in network events that are not going to be worthwhile for you.

At the event

One of the important things that you need to have in mind is that you go to a networking event for two reasons. One is to get information; at the event, you will be in learning mode. While listening, you can evaluate if you are able to add value to the topic being addressed. Another reason is to meet people. You usually go to an event in the Silicon Valley to talk to the people that you don't know instead of investing your time with the people that you already know. If you already know them, you have access to them, to call them back over the phone, invite them to drink coffee or to have a meeting with them to discuss ideas. But the people that usually get into the events are very much seeking to explore new connections.

After the event

After an event, it is important to look back at the connections you've just made and evaluate them. Is this person going to be useful for your activities in the short term? Or do you want to establish this contact for possible reference in the future? For the people that you are interested in maintaining contact with, you want to follow up and find a way of connecting. This step is quite important. Don't just file away business cards—make sure you follow up so that your time talking to these people was invested wisely.

Most people know to follow up on contacts, but don't forget to follow up on the "learning" portion of the event. A very helpful exercise would be to ask, "What did I learn that I found interesting?" I really encourage you to do this and don't just think about it, but write it out and even post it to your blog. This will allow you to look back at how you are using your time and what value you are getting out of these events. If you are posting this to a blog, you are sharing your expertise with a lot of people and perhaps reminding people you met about you. You are visible to them. They can reach you, not only now in the events, but at other times as well.

Finding Your Innovational Space

How can you find an ideal innovational space? Identify which events and people have been the most valuable for you. What are the places where you get great information, where interesting people get together, where you can really keep going to move forward with your ideas? If you are building your own company, the things that will be important to you are: loyalty, marketing, financial resources. If you have your product already on the market and you want to keep going, maybe the valuable areas for you will be how to provide better support that is cheaper and higher quality. The focus of your innovational spaces may change over time because you focus on different stages within your company as it grows.

CHAPTER 4

Fostering Local Incubation: From Idea to Business Model

Big ideas will never be anything more than that without the right amount of incubation time. Many think that the Silicon Valley would be a perfect place to build a new company. But that is a tough game—the Silicon Valley is one of the most expensive areas in the world. It is a very sophisticated environment and sometimes you are not ready to dive in with a fledgling company.

You want to create a company that is going to be global in the sense that you may be selling around the world. But the incubation period is a time for your local environment and you should take advantage of the resources around you. Every company starts somewhere small, but with the following concepts, you'll be able to use the Silicon Valley mindset to create a business model, without needing to be there physically (at least the whole time).

For the incubation period, I had been using a combination of two different approaches from the Silicon Valley. From the discovery side, a set of tools based on the Innovation Games Methodology, an interactive method created by Luke Hohmann. This approach allows you to evaluate and get feedback from your customers in a very easy way, in a fun and relaxed environment. A second approach is the Lean Startup Methodology created by Eric Ries, derived from work done by Steve Blank. Using the combination of these two tools you can create in two steps a good road map to really focus and build that great idea that you have already identified. To help guide your building, we have developed an eight-step process that is very easy to follow.

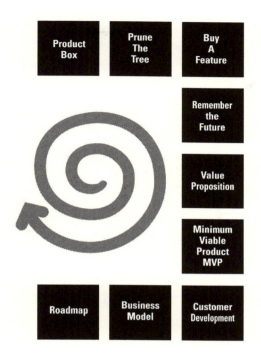

Tools to convert ideas into a Road Map

Step One—Product Box

Product Box is a training methodology where you gather people from different backgrounds related to your technology, area of expertise, and market, to get initial feedback on your idea. Start by creating materials for a demonstration. Sure you don't have an actual product yet, but for your presentation describe the features and main characteristics, the price, how to use it, and what you expect the market for this product to be. Gather together a group of people who can provide intelligent and constructive comments. You will get helpful feedback on your idea in just a few hours, instead of going through the whole product development process first. You may get positive reactions showing you that you are on the right track. You could learn that you have too many unnecessary features that will hold back your launch. Sometimes, the Product Box process reveals a complex problem before it is too late.

Step Two—Prune the Tree

There are two financial approaches to building a product and it is important that you choose one early in the process. If you want to meet a certain price point for your product, you have to set a limit for yourself and work back from there. Discuss with your team the features that you find essential and those that are secondary. That way, you can work to include the features that are important without going over the desired price for the customer.

A second choice is to allocate an overall budget for the project and to develop based on that. You estimate and define how much it will cost to build each one of the features you want to include. You can then create a list to prioritize the features you want that will allow you to stay within the budget you have created.

Step Three—Press Release

The next stage of your process is to write a press release, assuming its publication for the time that you will launch your product. Yes, your product is barely off the ground; but this will allow you to have a vision of the future. This exercise will let you think about a time frame for your project, as well as how the product will be described to the market. Keep this press release on hand so that you have a clear idea of the future that you want to accomplish. Referring to this will make it easier for the whole team to be in the same mindset. This is a unique way to align visions from all the participants in the project.

Step Four—Value Proposition

Taking all the information from the last three steps, you can refine your value proposition. A very simple way to review your value proposition is to ask, "What would be the minimum necessary for this to be a valuable product for your market?" Using this product you've described, you can gather even more feedback. Create websites and a hook marketing campaign online; reach people through newsletters, LinkedIn, Google AdWords, and all other kinds of channels that you have in your toolbox.

Step Five—Listen and Revise

Once you start spreading the word to the customer and getting responses, you will start to fine tune. Try to get in contact with these trial customers to see what they expect from a product like this, what features they want to use, what they felt was unnecessary. Some will probably be excited and ready to have it right way; other people may not give you any feedback; and there are those that will be providing some ideas that may help you change your product for the better.

The point to keep in mind is that you will be creating several iterations of your product and this exercise will allow you to define a much clearer value proposition. Once you hear from customers, create a new minimum valuable product, and develop a new campaign. You may do this several times until you really have a great product to move forward with. Or you may realize there is no market for this product or the approach to it is all wrong. Either way, you will have saved yourself a lot of time and money finding out at this stage.

Step Six—Create a Business Model

After you have gone through the first five steps, you will have feedback, data, and a very clear idea of what you want to build. It is time to create a business model. I won't take you through the whole process here; that is a whole book topic on its own. But if you want a great interactive approach, I would recommend the Business Model Generation system created by Alex Osterwalder. You can find his simple and creative steps in the book *Business Model Generation* or in the interactive online Business Model Toolbox on his website. You will use the information you have gathered up to this point and further define your market and the revenue model that you are going to follow.

Step Seven—Road Map

You can write a business model in a couple of days and then you will have the base to build your road map. This is going to be the guide for how you are going to build your product and reach the market. Be specific with the steps to take and what resources you'll need. Depending on the product's characteristics and complexity, your road map could cover months or years. Don't be daunted—this will keep your team on the right track and provide guidelines when coming up against problems.

Step Eight—Visit the Valley

Even if you cannot start your company in the Silicon Valley, it would be beneficial for you to experience it as part of your process. Your local environment may offer you many resources, but it may also be lacking others. If you are able to, try to arrange a visit to the Silicon Valley in order to take advantage of some of its unique characteristics. Networking there would obviously be a crucial part of your trip. It is possible you will be able to meet potential customers or investors. You may find another company to create an alliance with in order to get your product on the market faster. No matter what, you will be able to make connections with people with different viewpoints.

Not sure how to begin or who to talk to there? Try reaching out to members of the various Silicon Valley professional organizations in your industry. Perhaps you can find a program that will guide your visit and arrange meetings. For instance, I offer my clients a 10-day mentorship bootcamp so that they can learn from the environment and bring it back to their new company. Of course this includes access to the networking events we talked about in a previous chapter. But another benefit to a program like this is access to the other participants. Usually, we are working with clients all around the world, so participants are coming from places as diverse as Mexico and Finland to Australia and Argentina. We have group sessions for the participants to discuss their ideas and what they've learned, which open the doors to even more diverse mindsets and connections. Finding like-minded entrepreneurs is a great way to focus your trip and learn from diverse people.

CHAPTER 5

Landing in a New Place: Finding the Right Ecosystem

Starting a local company is fairly straightforward. You have a great product and you tailor it to local needs that you are very familiar with since you share in that environment. But in this book, we are focusing on how you create an innovative **global** company, meaning you have some level of income from abroad and your company is known around the world.

It is time to go beyond your own backyard. You can't become a global company if you are only trying to sell to people within a 50-mile radius. Creating a company that meets local needs is great, but if you think locally all the time you will find yourself very limited by the market. That is going to be a big problem if you want to grow your company and expand it.

If you currently have a successful local company, why would you want to expand? Consider the way customers shop today. Even people in small towns have access to products from all around the world. Online shopping means that just about anything is just a click away.

One of the most common questions I get when working with companies is, "Why do I need to be aware of what is going on in my industry in other parts of the world?" Often, local companies believe they offer such a great service to their area that they don't need to worry about the global competition. They believe their customers are loyal and won't be swayed. But this is a miscalculated view.

Your company cannot afford to be ignorant of its global competitors. You should certainly be able to identify who your competitors are, where they are located, and what features they have that you can't offer now. Customers faced with lower prices, exciting features, or better service may not be as loyal as you assume them to be. You must not let your company become stagnant; innovation is what got you success in the market and it needs to continue. This will enable you to start thinking globally and with the goal of expanding.

I realize that this isn't so easy. I remember in a recent conference, someone said it is very hard to think globally and act locally. That phrase has been around for a while, but it is a crucial one. I told him, "It is true that it is hard to do both those things, but isn't it also hard to watch your company going down the drain?" This is a different kind of world and you need to decide if you want your company to last. If you do, you can use your local foothold to your advantage as you plan your move to the global market.

Act Locally: What Can You Learn Right Here?

Your current local customers are an excellent resource for market research. Start communicating with them to find out what they see as your strengths. Why do they buy your products or use your services? What things do they like? What do they wish was better? What do they see as unique to their local area?

There are many areas in which you may excel: in your product development, in your raw materials, in the capability to be very creative, in your speed to release a product, or your significant human resources. You may also serve very unique kinds of needs for this local environment. This information from the customer's point of view could really help you design and implement products in a better way. You can start doing that in your local environment and apply those lessons as you expand.

Think Globally: Where Should I Go?

Maybe you do not need to be convinced that you ought to expand globally. Perhaps you are ready and your question really is: *where* should I expand? Landing in the right ecosystem for your company is one of the most important challenges that you need to solve. You might expect me to say that you should run to the Silicon Valley and see how people do things. This could be beneficial if you are looking to have a very daring and trying test of your business.

But that is not necessarily the best choice for your company. You need to find where in the world is the best place for your kind of product or services to be developed. If you are in retail maybe a place like Arkansas where Walmart is located; if you are in heavy industry, maybe the Northeast of the United States would be ideal; if you are in finance, why not go to London; if you are doing something in the food industry perhaps San Francisco, California can be a great niche market for you.

Finding the most developed place for your industry is crucial and that is something you need to identify. A lot of people think that if they go into a place that is the top of their industry it will be very tough because the companies there are the best ones in the world. That's the whole idea! When you are just beginning to expand you need to learn and where better than an environment that is ideal to your industry?

The important thing to consider is that even if you are in the same area, you don't necessarily need to compete head to head. An example that I love to remind people of is Google. When Google started, they were not considered to be a competitor of Microsoft. They were in the Internet search industry and Microsoft was barely involved in it at all. Fifteen years later, Google is one of the strongest competitors in three areas that are major components of Microsoft: operating systems, tools like e-mail and office productivity and of course, search. Sometimes you need to start small and focus on what makes your company unique. Perfecting your strengths could lead to you going into other segments or to you being acquired by another company that is expanding. In any case, you don't need to start out being all things to all people.

A good way to test out a potential market for expansion is to find some help to perform a "soft landing" in the new location. After you've done some research, you may find a location that seems ideal as a new market for your company. This isn't necessarily going to be in another country; it could simply be the next state over. Send an exploration team to start learning essential things about this new environment.

Here are some logistical and practical issues they should be discovering:

1. **Legal—Know the Rules**
   Before you can do anything to expand into a new territory, you must be well informed on the laws of that area. Do you need a local branch in order to distribute your product in this country? Even if that is not the case, perhaps having knowledgeable people on the ground will save you a lot of time and money in navigating the local laws. In addition, if you are in a different country, then you should be aware of any international laws and regulations that will apply.

2. **Networking—Ask the Locals**
   I have talked before about the importance of networking. It will be all the more crucial as you move your business to a new environment. A very common thing in most towns is the Chamber of Commerce. These organizations are concerned with the local businesses and promoting them to the local environment. This will allow you to learn more about the place and meet

residents. Try to find out if there are local business organizations for your industry. Or perhaps there are chapters of national or international organizations that hold events in that area. Endeavor to make contacts in your own industry or those that could be potential customers. Having local contacts to help you find resources and establish yourself will be extremely helpful.

3. **Sales—Cultural Norms Matter**

    The Sales Department is an essential, yet extremely complicated, element of your company. It doesn't matter how good your product is if no one knows about it or if it is being presented to them in a way they don't understand. Perhaps you have a great local sales team now. But you can't just barge into a new place and expect people to have the same cultural norms or values that you have. The best way to get local knowledge is to merge with the local people. Our first recommendation to the companies that come to expand their business is to build a two person team; one person comes from your company (perhaps it is even you), and partners with a local person from the same business area. This approach speeds up the introduction of your company into the local business. In business and sales, there are cultural values that you must be aware of to smooth your expansion into this market. People from one place may find face-to-face contact necessary, while people from another place may want everything to be available online. The local contacts you have established through networking will be essential in helping you navigate these situations.

4. **Finances—Follow the Money**
   The financial environment in this new place could also present challenges, so be sure it is investigated early. Start with banking and credit cards. Do you need a local checking account? What about local credit cards? Also consider the kinds of insurance coverage you need to limit your liabilities. Do you need investors? How do you get involved with the local venture capital companies and is there anything you need to understand about the process here? It is important to cover all the financial bases in your initial research or you could run into some expensive problems.

5. **Support—Cover All the Bases**
   There are of course many other issues that you ought to consider depending on the type of business you are in. Are there regulations in terms of packaging or warning labels? Are there local telecommunications restrictions that you should be aware of? The list could go on and on. Usually, the best way of covering all your bases would be to hire a support company that is familiar with this type of project. Local support can help you identify issues about your facility, location, tax laws, government regulations, and compliance. In the Silicon Valley for instance, there are more than 115,000 one to five person business, small consulting firms, and fully structured organizations that provide services like these from business consulting to environmental testing for specific products or materials. In the local environment that you are landing in, you need to identify these companies and what services you need. As part of your "soft

landing" it is very important that you select the best resources to get your company established.

Map Out Your Journey

So are you ready to land abroad? Then you need a plan to get you there. You need to define where you plan to go, why you want to be there and assign a set of resources to accomplish the goal that you want to achieve. Even if you know all this in your head, make a definitive document. Describe why you want to expand into this market. Is it to reach a new market, to find potential business alliances, or to develop products tailored to different local needs? Also, establishing what resources you want to devote to this goal will help you to stay reasonable. Be smart about your plan and try to reach the market with the least amount of necessary resources.

The most important element of your plan will be your timeline. If you don't set the goals in a timeline, you are setting yourself up to drift indefinitely. This is very dangerous because no matter what size company you are, your capabilities and your resources are always limited. Be sure each step of your plan has a clear date attached. As your expansion progresses, include the timeline in your evaluation process. Don't allow your project to go completely off track.

Once you have a plan, you will need help implementing it. In the next chapter, I will discuss how to build the right team.

CHAPTER 6

Pre-Operation Stage: Getting Ready to Do Business Abroad

You've already come a long way in your quest to be a KING. You have a great product and a great local company. Now you are almost ready to take your business to the next level. After the last chapter, you should have the tools to jump in and do business abroad (or at least outside of where you are located originally). But let's consider a few more logistical concerns of such a jump.

You will be facing one of the biggest challenges yet to this new company. You have already gotten through the initial challenges: having a great idea, creating an integrated product, testing how people react to it. Now you must face the complications of setting up shop in a new place. Doing this in your same country could be easier but that is not necessarily to say that is going to be an easy job. If you decide to jump far away and go outside your own country, seek a place where your capabilities are the best fit. As we discussed in the last chapter, you should go to a new place, be it a neighbor or on the other side of the world, where your capabilities have a competitive advantage and a great differentiation.

Putting Together the Right Team

Now you must face how to actually be in two locations at the same time. You want to keep a firm foundation in your original location but you also want the expansion to succeed. In your local environment you have the advantages of knowledge of the area and a great team of people that support you. How can you build that in the new location? Just as you did when you built your company initially, you need to find people to fill in the skills that you or the company lack. You may have to reorganize your original team in order to have people that can maintain a connection between locations. Of course you need to keep your most valuable people hard at work, but you need to choose who is going to be the ambassador for you in new location. Think about who knows your company very well: how it operates, how it has been able to be successful locally, what special capabilities make it unique. This person will also need to have courage and the ability to empathize with people in this new place. You also need to be sure the new location has strong leadership. You will need to establish someone in the new location who can lead effectively.

You can send your brightest and bravest, but there is still a lot you will need to know that will be impossible for someone from the outside to understand. In the new location you have the challenge of building a new team that will provide you with the kind of local experience and support that you have back home. Don't think you can wait until you are established and *then* hire local employees. You need local people from the very beginning to help you. They will be better equipped to help you to find and communicate with customers and navigate the many obstacles we discussed in the last chapter.

Your two teams will have very different roles. The employees that are in your original location are able to maintain your products and develop new projects. The new location should have employees that are skilled at finding new customers and providing support. The new location should work to promote your company in the new market. Giving demonstrations and trial service could help them prove to potential customers that you are the best solution for them. Despite the different roles, your locations should clearly be a unified company. Make sure that the interface between the two groups is set up well from the beginning.

Take the Time to Evaluate

Once you get a great team in the new location, they will set to work doing promotion, talking to the customers, and trying to nail down opportunities and close on sales. That first sale is really one of the biggest successes that you can have. This is a brand new market for you and your potential customers don't really know what to expect from you. This is the opportunity to show them what your company is about. It is also a great opportunity for you to learn from them.

One of the most important jobs for the team in your new location will be evaluating customer feedback and the local market. First they can talk to satisfied customers to see what they appreciate about your product, your company or your customer support. The evaluators on your team should be working to draw out these customers and find out if you are meeting the expectations they had. Just as important, is to talk to dissatisfied customers, to discover what can be improved to make their experience better.

In addition to customer evaluations, there should be a regular evaluation of your business abroad. Take a hard look at whether this expansion is worthwhile—is it generating enough business, profits, opportunities, and room for more growth? If this additional location or market is not serving to make your business stronger, you must be able to know why.

Your customer evaluations paired with your business analysis will help you make adjustments to your company as needed. You may look at the data and decide this venture was really just an experiment and didn't go well. I hope, however, that you will find that this was the best decision for your company. With the invaluable knowledge and experience you've gained from this expansion, you can continue to grow your company into new markets.

CHAPTER 7

Acquiring New Customers: Getting Traction in the Market

Setting up a new location isn't much good without customers. Now that you are established, you will need to gain traction in your new market. There are a number of ways of getting customers, though not all of them are all that effective. Here is an overview, starting with the worst methods and working up to the best.

1. **Advertising**
   Traditional advertising, both print and television, is very difficult for a new company. Getting your brand established through advertising can be nearly impossible in today's overly saturated media. This method is cumbersome and expensive and not very recommended for new companies.

2. **Trade Shows**
   Trade shows or expos are another way of attracting customers. You can buy a booth and have a presence at the show. If you are lucky the right people will stop by to talk to you. It is possible for real potential customers to find you there, but it relies on your materials attracting their attention.

3. **Telemarketing**
   One of the traditional methods of finding new customers is through telemarketing. You create telemarketing material, find a qualified list of people, and create, or hire, a call center. This approach very much depends on luck. Usually, even if you get the right people on the phone, you usually only have about a 2% success rate in getting a meeting with them.

4. **Website**
   In today's business world, it is essential to have an online presence. First of all, you need a well-executed website that is very attractive and contains helpful information. Be sure that you get set up with analytics software, so you can track your visitors. Tools like Google Analytics not only can tell you how many visitors came

to your website, but also how they arrived there (online search, link from another website, typing in the address directly), what city they live in, how long they spent on the website and how many pages they visited.

5. **Blogs**
Your website should have a blog. It allows you to constantly have fresh updated content and additional opportunities for search engines to find you. You can also connect with other bloggers who write about your industry. Bloggers are the new press contacts; you will be far more likely to get publicity on a blog than in traditional publications. If a popular blog writes up your product or company, it can generate a lot of traffic to your website. This in turn could lead to new customers.

6. **Social Networks**
Social networks can also help you make contacts. LinkedIn, for instance, can help you find the people in the right positions in a company that you are targeting. You can see if you have any shared contacts that can make an introduction for you. You can also have Facebook pages or Twitter feeds for your company. If you are involved in a big event or trade show, be sure to include these things on your materials so that people can keep up with the company news. It can be a challenge to build up followers, but like your blog, it can be an excellent source of information for potential customers.

7. **Networking Events**
Attending networking events is one of the greatest ways to go. These events allow you to meet people

face-to-face. As you talk to them and explain what are you doing, they may be able to introduce you to the right people. By "right people" I don't necessarily mean customers, but also those who can be good business alliances and expose you to different distribution channels. Attending events also helps you to become part of the local community. If you are showing up regularly, you will speak to many people. As I said in an earlier chapter, try to introduce people to others you know who can help them. This will make them more receptive to hearing about your work and reciprocating the introduction. You can also use resources like meetup.com to create your own local events that are tailored to your interests. This is a great way to find the people in the area that are interested in the things you are working on.

8. **Speaking At Events**

    One of the best ways to get interested potential customers to contact you is to be a speaker at an event. This could be a small networking meeting or a large conference; being a speaker shows that you know how to solve problems people are interested in. It isn't so much about selling but showing you to be an expert. In the Silicon Valley it is common for organizations like SVForum (formerly known as Software Development Forum) or TiE Global to hold demo days that allow you to present your product and to pitch in front of investors. This kind of event gets the word out about your product and often it could be picked up by blogs or other industry-specific media.

9. **Extreme Marketing: The Lean Startup Approach**
   The final method I call the lean startup approach. Within our organization we call it extreme marketing. The extreme marketing concept is very similar to what you do in a "hackathon," where people get together to create marketing campaigns and value propositions using tools like Facebook. It is up to you whether you want to have your full network helping you with proposals or to have that be in a closed environment with a small group of people that can provide feedback about your ideas. Either way you learn how your proposal can be improved to create this value proposition. You then take this proposition and build an experiment design in how to reach customers. This is an approach that is good when you don't know who or where your potential customers are. You take your guesses about this and create a hypothesis for your experiment. Hopefully this experiment will create a funnel of prospects for your conversion process. Convert the people that are interested in your product through the distribution channel you have set up. You are ready to really start generating demand.

If you use these tools, you can start generating demand in the new market. It may be slow at first, but once you start closing sales you should get a reputation among customers in the area. This will get the ball rolling for the next steps in your expansion.

CHAPTER 8

Acceleration and Scaling: Awareness, Sales and Growth

If your initial experiments in expansion are succeeding, you may be ready to accelerate to the next level. The scalability of your business is a measure of its ability to rapidly expand without major disruptions or losses in profitability. Scaling your business is a complex stage; it is important to take the time to do it the right way.

In their book *Nail It Then Scale It*, Paul Ahlstrom and Nathan Furr explain that this stage is where many businesses fail; often the failure is due to trying to scale up too soon. This can be a difficult thing to determine. On the one hand, you do not want to invest heavily, enter many markets, overproduce your goods, and be left with product on the shelf. On the other hand, if the demand for your goods is outweighing your ability to produce, you may lose potential customers and sales. You need to scale at just the right time, when you have the capabilities and demand to expand rapidly.

It would be wise to plan for scaling long before you start. You must have a vision in advance of how to build your capabilities to withstand this expansion. Managing your supply chain is critical. The supply chain provides your raw materials and products and it is essential that you and the people in the chain have clear expectations of what scaling up will entail. There can be some major negotiations involved, to ensure that the supply chain can provide enough resources without overproducing. You must balance many factors and this will require a lot of business maturity. Are you ready for that?

You are undoubtedly good at what you do or you wouldn't have been able to launch a successful product. But the approaches that have worked for you so far are completely different from those needed to properly scale up your company. Often people believe that money is the solution to acceleration like this and seek out investors. But money alone may not be enough; at times it can even be harmful if it causes you to scale too quickly.

The real question you need to ask yourself is: "Are you the right person to scale your company?" Most likely you started this company because you had a technology background and had a great idea for a product. Throughout the whole process you have known to bring people on board with the expertise that you lack. In this case, perhaps the best thing to do would be to bring someone into the company that has gone through a similar expansion.

This isn't always so easy to do; in your town, how many people do you know that have launched a product from scratch? How many of these people have handled all the production, the market and the financial resources needed? It is important to find someone who has scaled up a business to guide you through it. In that respect, being in the Silicon Valley can be a major benefit.

I've already discussed that many people in the Silicon Valley are open to failure and willing to take risks. Someone who has worked there may be a good resource to guide you, but the Silicon Valley is not necessarily the market to expand into first. A competitor could arise from nowhere with much better knowledge of how to scale and you may not be able to respond fast enough. Finding the right markets to expand into is an essential part of your planning process. I've talked a bit about this in the last couple chapters, but it is even more crucial as you scale up.

Your team is more important than ever at this juncture. You must be ready to meet all the challenges and have people designated to lead and manage different aspects of the expansion. The production, sales, support, and financial elements are all vital. Your staff must be well trained and ready to adapt to changing factors in the process. In that sense, human resources will also play a critical role in finding the right people at the right time.

These fives areas, production, sales, support, financial and human resources, have to be in place and part of a written plan. This plan for scaling can then be presented to potential investors. You need a clear view of how your acceleration will proceed into new markets, how your supply chain will be managed and how your current financial resources match up to these plans. You can approach potential venture capital firms that relate to your industry or future locations. You will need investments to pay your key employees and so they will have enough resources to start the expansion. If you don't have the capital, keeping things running smoothly at first is going to be very tough. If any of the areas stop working efficiently, it can disrupt your entire operation. You can have the best sales team in the world, but if the production process has slowed, customers will not have the products they've purchased. Or, the customers may have the products in hand, but when they have complaints or technical issues, there is not enough support staff to address their concerns. When one part stops functioning, you run into very big problems.

You have built your scalability capability and determined the plan for moving forward. Now you must ask yourself, where do you want to be in the future? Perhaps the challenge of scaling is not one that interests you and you would rather be a serial entrepreneur. You could step down and remain in a technical group or sit on the board. You could even sell the company altogether. Then you will be free to come up with new ideas and leave somebody else to run the company. On the other side, you can stay to build and continue to lead your company like Bill Gates. You can retire much later and pursue new projects, philanthropy, or mentorship of people who started out like you did.

When you started you found somebody that helped you. Now you are in a position where you have a huge amount of knowledge from your experiences. This allows you to generate great ideas, help people and teach them how to create a new venture. You can serve as a mentor or an investor helping them jump to the next level with their ideas. This will perhaps be the best thing you do since you accomplished something and through your success you can help many others to succeed as well.

| Product Box | Prune The Tree | Buy A Feature |

| | | Remember the Future |

Part III
What Makes Silicon Valley Work

CHAPTER 9

Role Models Are Not Enough: The Value of Meta Mentors

Andy Grove, co-founder of Intel, wrote an interesting article in *Businessweek* about corporate mentorship.[2] He discussed Intel's "technical assistants," who are employees paired with senior executives to provide mutual benefit. Grove notes that he gave them "seasoning" by helping

---

2   Grove, Andy. "Andy Grove: How to Be a Mentor." *Businessweek*. September 22, 2011. (http://www.businessweek.com/magazine/andy-grove-how-to-be-a-mentor-09222011.html)

them learn how to approach the kinds of hurdles they would encounter in the field. In turn, they educated him on a variety of industry innovations, including ideas about branding, networking and Internet applications. This is a great program, but there is some personal magic to it. He says, "Some stuff in companies can be made routine and machine-like. But teaching? You routinize it, you screw it up." He worried that by standardizing what is essentially a teaching role, human resources departments were going to ruin the whole concept.

Finding the right mentor can be a difficult endeavor. Who will be the best person to guide you? What can you contribute to help them? I find the best way is to start by defining a challenge or problem you are hoping to solve. Define your question and then think about the type of people that have the specific background to work on the solution. You may already know what I am going to say about this: the key is networking. Seek out events where these types of people will be and your mentor may come to you.

Finding the Right Person

Once again, being in the Silicon Valley makes this step very easy. Why? Because you have hundreds of events every year and the people who would be great mentors usually like to be speakers and members of panels. They like to be exposed to new people. Like you, your ideal mentor is a person seeking problems to be solved in new ways. Finding your mentor will probably take some effort. Maybe you are very lucky and your mentor will be just around the corner. But sometimes, you will have to search across the world.

As I've said before, in-person networking events are ideal. But even if you don't have the time or resources to attend events all over the world, you can still be on the lookout for potential mentors. Social networking sites are great sources for initial points of contact. LinkedIn for instance, is a great tool for finding people in specific industries or companies. It also allows you to see contacts you have in common that could initiate an introduction.

Making Contact

Once you have identified some potential mentors, the next step is how to approach them. At networking events, you have to imagine that they are talking to dozens of people. How can you make an impression that is going to capture your potential mentor's attention? You need to create a great elevator pitch that describes your challenge and how this person could be the perfect person to help you solve it. The goal is to spark a discussion that they will want to come back to. Usually at an event like this, you don't have that much time to talk with one person. Trigger his interest and then ask to talk more with him later. Ask for a business card and move on to other people.

Later, send your potential mentor a more substantial e-mail, reminding him of your meeting at the event. Describe your challenge again in more detail, and ask him to be part of a mentorship project. Your e-mail should not overly flatter, but should indicate how this person is uniquely qualified to lend their expertise to your problem. Be clear about the specific things you would expect from this relationship and what areas of your challenge you think he could particularly contribute to.

What's In It For Them?
Another crucial part of this exchange is you need to identify the potential mentor's motivation. Will this person be excited about your challenge and consider the solution to be a reward in itself? Perhaps as someone with a huge amount of experience in the industry, he will see this as an entertaining way to give back to the community. Other kinds of mentors will be looking for some compensation for the work done. Remember that compensation does not have to mean money. A typical way these situations happen in the Silicon Valley is that you invite this person to be your mentor as a CEO or CTO. In exchange for helping to solve this problem, the company provides them with some stock. As a fledgling company, perhaps those stocks are not worth anything at all right now. This type of compensation is really proof that your mentor is confident in this project because he is betting on your success. If you ask for something, be prepared to define a reward to be given back. Be sure that reward is clear and that both of you have the same expectations from the beginning.

Reciprocal Benefits
The ideal mentorship situation will involve reciprocal benefits and learning. As Andy Grove noted, sometimes it is hard to tell just who is mentor and who is mentee. This two-way learning experience is vitally important and will hopefully help you both achieve your goals.

If you are seeking out a mentor, be sure you are really willing to receive their mentorship. Remember, you as a mentee are usually going to be working much harder than the mentor. If your mentor doesn't feel you are devoting a lot of time and effort to this project, they will not have much interest in it. Have clear, achievable goals; when you achieve one of them, it is important to recognize the accomplishment and celebrate it with your team and mentor. If you fail, it is also important to understand why and how to modify things when you try again. Use your mentor as a resource to understand where things went wrong; definitely do not blame them for your failure. Even if they didn't provide you as much help as you wanted, the person ultimately responsible for your success is you. That is one of the entrepreneurship rules that you need to always keep in mind.

Meta Mentors—Teaching the Teachers

Beyond traditional mentorships, there is a category of people who I call "Meta Mentors." These are the people who help build the mentoring capability in other people. I am really surprised that there is so little research or articles on this subject, because it is so crucial.

One of my greatest conversations I ever had was with Héctor García-Molina, a professor at Stanford University. He grew up in Mexico and came to the US to get his PhD at Stanford University. Héctor and I met a long time ago and I really respect his point of view because he is such a clever and humble guy. We had dinner recently and I asked him, "You have been the mentor of some great people (the creators of Yahoo and Google, for instance), so what is the process you chose to be a mentor?" I really enjoyed his face at that moment. He said, "Jorge, you really like to ask challenging questions." For me, that was a great moment, because I was having a discussion with someone so knowledgeable and successful and he says that it is a challenge to talk to me. That is the key to a great mentor relationship: a mutually challenging environment.

During dinner we tried to analyze how exactly PhD students are guided by their thesis advisors. There is very little discussion around this idea, which is pretty strange in the scientific fields where testing and proof of a concept is so important. Héctor told me that he's been advising students for almost 30 years as a professor, but he could not explain right away his process. Although it is something he knows very well how to do and repeats year after year, he could not provide me a simple and structured recipe or process.

This is a really important concept, especially when trying to replicate the Silicon Valley environment. Mentors aren't born knowing what to do; someone else has taught them to be a mentor, probably without ever realizing what they were doing. These are the Meta Mentors. I asked Héctor how a new professor is trained to be a great mentor like him. He said recently he suggested they start to have a program to teach these professors how to be mentors. This is an excellent way to make this an explicit type of teaching.

After that dinner, I thought about the different kinds of mentors and role models I have had over the years. I realized that my life has been full of great mentors. Some have come from my hobbies and others from my professional life. I found that my mentors usually lasted for a given period of time; it was not the same amount each time, but there was always an end point to the relationship as mentors, becoming great peers. The mentorship process seemed to follow a pattern of meeting, learning from their experience, developing into a mutual learning environment, and then transitioning into a less active relationship as I grew and changed. The relationship of the master and apprentice is unique; the dream of the master is that the apprentices surpass you. Hopefully you may end up being a mentor of your mentor—that will be the highest achievement that you can accomplish. In that same *Businessweek* article, Andy Grove really captured the mentor relationship. He says, "Did I mentor them? They taught me as much as I taught them. So who is the mentor and who is the mentee? Is "mentee" a real word? I hate it."

The Mentor role for an entrepreneur is so invaluable. The approach that is described in the corporate environment is much more important for an entrepreneur that does not have the resources to convert a crazy idea into an enterprise. Therefore, the entrepreneur needs to find how to challenge a mentor by presenting the project in an attractive way. This should be enough to involve the mentor in finding the solution that is based in a raw idea that will be nurtured into a good solution. Once the idea is molded into a full solution that reaches the market and produces returns that make a business, the mentor is able to be rewarded. The hope with stocks of the company is that some day you can cash out and become a billionaire as a lot of the successful companies in the Silicon Valley have managed to do. As it has happened to hundred of entrepreneurs that ask for help from an experienced person that they meet in an event, entrepreneur César Salazar met David Weekly in a SVForum event. At that time César was looking for guidance to build a web application known as d.oing.it, that was meant to help people to manage tasks and "to-do" lists. David helped César and his team to build this project; it was built and tested in the market but they found that they were not able to convert it into a business. From the mentorship, César and his team learned how to build applications, but they wanted to go further. They decided to move forward as Meta Mentors and move from doing their own projects to helping people in Mexico learn how to launch products locally. This experience transformed César and his partner Santiago into venture capitalists and they founded Mexican.VC. In doing so, they are helping others to do what they learned from their mentor.

CHAPTER 10

Last Chapter, First Step: Believing You Can Do It

One of the nicest parts of being in the Silicon Valley is that you look around and see how big companies really grow from a simple idea. This has happened time and again with companies like Hewlett Packard, Apple, or Google. These companies all started with just a couple guys with a big idea and the will to make it happen. How can you be part of this?

All these companies started when they identified a good opportunity to solve a problem in the market. They were able to use their skills to solve those problems. Strong leadership is crucial to that opportunity becoming a real company. You must be the person that connects the dots and bring together the people who can take you further. Your leadership and strong networking skills will help you find the person to help you with marketing or the person that is going to invest in your company. You need to keep going until you find all the elements that you need to bring that idea into the market.

Money should not be your main issue. A true entrepreneur is the person that is able to produce results even without having many resources. That is a very big difference between you and an executive in a big company. The executive has usually been granted a lot of resources that he must leverage in order to bring back the desired results to stockholders. The entrepreneur on the other hand must only report to himself and keeps his own drive moving. But you must believe in yourself and your ability to achieve your goals. For every goal you set and achieve, you will find there is another challenge to be solved. The next challenge will define where you go next. It can be difficult to navigate at times, but if you have a clear vision of where you are headed, it will be easier to get there. Many people dream of going to places no one has ever gone to before; successful people dare to dream and believe that they can get there.

Usually, the entrepreneur is not able to do everything. There are some serial entrepreneurs that already have a huge amount of experience. But you will have your work cut out for you to get a new company started. If you have a great team around you, things are going to be much easier. Who should be part of this team? Perhaps you have a co-founder. This person is taking the same risk as you are and is dedicated to getting to the dream place that you set as a destination. You will undoubtedly have investors and advisors who are eager to see you succeed. Your team will include your main mentor, the person you can come to anytime to serve as a sounding board for your ideas. Have people on the team that you know can handle uncertainty—there will definitely be quite a bit in the early stages and you need to know who can help you deal with it. Asking for help can be tough for many entrepreneurs, but it is essential that you be able to rely on people around you. I can't emphasize enough that you must believe in yourself. If you have that confidence, that level of trust within you, you need to share that. Make sure the people on your team believe that you are going to achieve what you have set out to do.

If you are a building a company for the first time, particularly coming from abroad, you need to learn that you build great things one brick at a time. Thinking big is important, but things get accomplished by doing a little each day. Set clear goals that can be accomplished. Once they are complete, move on to the next and keep moving toward your end result. You must be able to communicate to your team what needs to be done to get to that far-off goal. If you want to have a million visitors to your website, start with the first 100 people. When you achieve the first 100 people, work towards 1000 people. As you progress, make sure those initial customers that are buying your product are having a great customer experience.

Along the way, you are going to fail. That may sound disheartening, but don't worry. Failure is a learning process; you accept that not everything is working as you planned and then you can adapt. That is why small steps are also important, because it is much easier to backtrack and get on the right course. You learn from failure, make the corrections, set a new course of action and you are still able to be moving forward. At this stage, you need the freedom to be nimble and adjust your course of action. Your team should trust your leadership and share your principles and plans for the future of the company. At the end of the day, you need to know your limitations. Perhaps at a certain stage you will realize that you are not the right person to be performing a certain role. Believing in yourself also means you can admit that you are not the best person for a task.

You need to remember how you started your journey. After you have gone through all these endeavors is the time to look back and enjoy your success. Your company shows what you are capable to build from an idea to a successful enterprise. The wealth created provides you a solid platform to live for a long time. Now is the time that you need to sit, see the future in a different way, and then be available to help, as a mentor, the next person behind you.

My friend, you have to enjoy the challenge. Building a company is a joy; seeing something you have worked so hard at achieve results is a major pleasure in life. When your dreams are achieved you can sit back and be satisfied that you did it.

APPENDIX

Acknowledgements

Writing this book is the result of seven great years of living in the Silicon Valley, jumping back and forth between the United States and many cities in Mexico. I have to acknowledge several people that made it possible, from the far seeing people that envisioned this program in the Mexican Government and the US-Mexico Foundation for Science. Unfortunately, to acknowledge all the people would require me to write the same amount of pages as this book.

From the Mexican government I want to thank Bruno Ferrari, the current Minister of Economy, who has encouraged me to find a better way to foster the creation of the best innovative companies, along with the support of Miguel Maron, current Under Secretary of the Small and Medium Enterprise in the Minister of Economy. Previously Sergio Garcia de Alba, former Minister of Economy who was a mentor and a boss, and Alejandro Gonzalez, former Under Secretary of the Small and Medium Enterprise in the Minister of Economy.

I also want to thank Jana Nieto, who oversaw the creation of the TechBA program inside the Minister of Economy. Jana has been a great supporter with a unique care for detail, always looking to be helpful and watching every single detail to improve the execution of the activities.

From the ProMexico side, Carlos Guzman, Jorge Lopez, Enrique Haro, Fernando Franco, Mario Juarez have been great partners supporting everyday activity.

Thanks go to FUMEC, our parent organization, led by Guillermo Fernandez, who is always seeking ways to make better programs, finding access for everybody, and match making to connect to people everywhere. From the Board of Governors I want to mention Leopoldo Rodriguez, Karl Ruggeberg, Bernard Robertson, Cipriano Santos and Mary Walshok who continuously helped me to find better ideas to be innovative. And thanks go especially to Leopoldo Rodriguez, who has helped to manage my disruptive spirit to create new ways of building value.

Thanks go to my counterparts and colleagues—Haru Yamasaki, Luis Medina, Raul Carvajal, Leoncio Salaburu, Federico Goroztieta, Eugenio Marin, Itzam de Gortari—who share a great passion for helping people to learn the way to land in new places.

I owe a debt of gratitude to Mariano Contreras, Ana Boeta, and Ivan Zavala for making available their huge network of entrepreneurs and companies in Mexico to help them find new boundaries and explore going abroad.

From Conacyt and private enterprises, thanks to Guillermo Aguirre and Gustavo delVillar for allowing me to pick their brains, bounce off new ideas, and test concepts. Victor Reyes helped me from his role in government to understand how to better help entrepreneurs and in his recent activity as a partner sharing ideas as co-founder of www.mexicoinnova.com, a blog that talks about innovation.

Thanks to Adriana Tortajada from NAFIN, Jaime Sanchez from MexicoVentures and Luis Antonio Marquez from Amexcap for helping me understands the Mexican venture capital environment and inviting me to foster its development.

Thanks to the Institute of Mexican Abroad for all the help received to connect to Mexicans around the world, asking them for their support and helping to build my mentoring network. I especially want to acknowledge Carlos Gonzalez Gutierrez, Annie Carrillo, Sofia Orozco, Federico Bass, Javier Diaz de Leon.YevgenyKuznetsov and Jean Louis Racine from the Worldbank that share great ideas to grab the Mexican Diaspora as a support for my day-to-day activities.

I am also thankful for the great support provided by all the people from the General Consulate of Mexico in San Jose. First, Bruno Figueroa who initially welcomed me lands in Silicon Valley. Then David Figueroa for his guidance on how to reach the high level of people in the Silicon Valley and Mexico, and currently Carlos Ponce, who is a great supporter and promoter of our activities. Also to Jose Eduardo Loreto, Jorge Agraz, and every single person in the Mexican Consulate, I can never express all my thanks for your many activities that supported us.

From the City of San Jose, there is a long list of people that have been part of our activities: Starting with Mayor Chuck Reed and the former Mayor Ron Gonzalez with their team Jeff Ruster, BJ Sims, Dhez Woodworth, Kim Walesh, Rosy Herrera, and Scott Green. They provided open access to teach us how we can build better bridges between Mexican companies and the local government, universities, and private enterprise.

This book would not exist without the invaluable help of my editor, Henry DeVries. It was amazing to me how he was able to help take many unconnected ideas and turn them into a solid way to share with the reader a structured path to go abroad.

Thanks to my team that has been supporting me all the way: Jose Mendez, Adolfo Tavera, Ana de la Vega, Adolfo y Mario Nemirovsky, Constanza Nieto, Simon Golbard, Isaac Majerowicz and hundreds of other people that participated in events, lectures, workshops, etc. Also, Thanks to great partners like Mark White, John Matthensen, Luke Hohman and Ron Schilling who help me to help the companies in the program.

From the NBIA, I want to thank Ana Grief, David Monkman and Thomas Strodtbeck for communicating the value that we provide to companies.

I have been able to interact with hundreds of companies. Thanks to Abel and Carla Hurtado, Margarita Rodriguez, Jose Antonio Gonzalez, Ralph Aceves, Miguel Angel Casillas, Carlos Guzman, Oscar and Luis Nunez, Fernando Sepulveda and so many others for your suggestions and feedback.

Thanks to my friends in the Silicon Valley and Seattle— Antonio Lopez, Natan Saad, Pedro Celis, Jose Blakeley, Bismarck and Belsasar Lepe—who have encouraged me to keep going all this time.

Gratitude also to friends like Raul Lucido, Luis Villegas, Juan Navarro, and Rafael Fernandez that in some time have worked with me and at other times shared great moments.

To the unique team of Innovimiento, Antonio Tajonar, Ana Garcia and Carolina Castelazo that show me how deal with innovation in enterprise in Mexico and land it into practical ways of work locally.

This is also a great place to acknowledge some of my mentors in the past: Jaime Palacios, Pedro Joselevich, and Guillermo Garza Galindo. I keep them in my heart as people that helped shape my professional career.

Moises Norena, Burton Lee, Hector Garcia Molina and David Nordfors great mentors that helped me design and build our mentoring programs to support entrepreneurs building innovation. Mauricio Brehm, Rafael Sosa, Mario Zavala that built in me the deep interest in developing people, the best asset that you find around you.

The greatest support I can acknowledge is from wife, Ana, and my two sons, Daniel and Santiago, who have been part of this entire endeavor, as they have supported in every moment my passion to work around the clock and delay vacations to execute programs while challenging me all the time with great questions and providing suggestions from a different perspective. I can honestly tell the reader, there is no biggest pleasure in life when you see your family growing faster than you, reaching new horizons in their lives and giving me back the opportunity of learning from them, how to build patience, accomplish the unaccomplishable, and making their dreams happen as if they were mine.

About the Author

From January 2005 to December 2011 Jorge A. Zavala was CEO of TechBA Silicon Valley. Since January 2012, Jorge holds the position of Chief Disruptive Officer (CDO) of TechBA.

In January 2005 Jorge founded TechBA Silicon Valley with the purpose of supporting the **discovery of new opportunities** by finding the knowledge to explore new markets and develop the skills to expand their company's business in the U.S. and beyond using five elements: Mentoring, a Total Sales Process, Marketing Strategies, developing an Effective Management Team and establishing a Business Development and Financial Process. TechBA Silicon Valley has provided services to more than 400 small and medium size Mexican companies in the last seven years.

Additionally, Jorge has been developing awareness of the available Mexico's IT and technology capabilities to build partnership and customer opportunities for them with American entrepreneurs. Jorge's network of partners extends to Latin America and Europe.

A natural linkage to foster the development of high value companies and wealth creation is the participation of Jorge in the Red de Talentos initiative that the Mexican Minister of Foreign Affairs has promoted through the Institute of Mexican Abroad (IME, from the name in Spanish Instituto de Mexicanos en el Extranjero)—http://www.redtalentos.gob.mx/. This initiative currently has 14 chapters around the world.

Jorge is a unique high tech entrepreneur combining the better of two worlds: technical knowledge and expertise in the fields of electronics and computer science with the development of innovation-related areas with the companies supported. Jorge's extensive experience includes being a venture capitalist, a creator of new ventures as well as a professional communicator in the field of executive business management.

With more than 35 years of management experience, he has been the founder and CEO of seven companies. Prior to joining TechBA Silicon Valley as CEO, he worked as an Associate Partner and CTO of Visionaria, a venture capital group that provides funding, consulting and coaching capabilities to IT companies.

Jorge received a BS in Electrical Engineering from Universidad La Salle, Mexico in 1979, and a MS in Mathematics from the University of Waterloo, Ontario, Canada in 1984.

His interests include Innovation and Adoption, Knowledge Management, Seed and Angel Investment, Executive Leadership, and Global Entrepreneurship.

Jorge has been a Guest Speaker at the prestigious Graduate Business School IPADE (www.ipade.mx) in Mexico City, from 2001 to 2004 on topics of Creating Virtual Communities for Business Environments, Enabling Innovation within Organizations, Deployment Strategy: the Knowing and Doing Gap and Collaborative Learning.

Jorge has published several papers related to "How the Diaspora is a tool for economic development" and "How to do Business with Innovation." Jorge is bilingual in Spanish and English.

About TechBA

Since 2005 TechBA has supported and advised Small and Medium Technology Enterprises (SMEs) to have rapid growth in Mexico and elsewhere. TechBA's network of eight offices located in the USA, Canada, and Europe provides the environment to explore, discover, and land in a new location to expand commercial activities.

The TechBA program has been sponsored by the Ministry of Economy and the United States-Mexico Foundation for Science (FUMEC). Thanks to the high importance of TechBA in the global markets, SMEs in different industrial sectors from the regions in Mexico with high innovation potential can achieve great benefits. TechBA has supported the creation of thousands of new high quality jobs, both directly and indirectly, in the production lines and specialized niches where Mexican SMEs are involved. It is part of the National Business Gazelle of the Undersecretary of SMEs in the Ministry of Economy (SE).

Mentoring Practices Around the World

Americas

Argentina
Global TechBridge
10 South Third St, 3rd Floor
San Jose, CA 95113
Adolfo Nemirovsky
adolfonemi@gmail.com
Ministry of Economic Development
Government of Buenos Aires
PO Box C1293 ABA 1041Algarrobo St
City of Buenos Aires, Argentina
Marcos Amadeo
(54-11)4126-2950 ext. 3065
mamadeo@buenosaires.gov.ar

Brazil
BayBrazil
508 Weybridge Drive
San Jose CA 95123

Margarise Correa
margarise@baybrazil.com

Canada
Consulate General of Canada, Silicon Valley
245 Lytton Avenue, 3rd Floor
Palo Alto, CA 94301
Thierry Weissenburger
Consul and Senior Trade Commissioner at our Consulate General in San Francisco
Thierry.Weissenburger@international.gc.ca
650-543-8800

Tab Borden
Consul and Senior Trade Commissioner at our Consulate General in San Francisco
Tab.Borden@international.gc.ca
(650) 543-8811
C100

Atlee Clark
Program Director
aclark@thec100.org
http://www.thec100.org

Ron Pioveson
Board Member
ronpioveson@gmail.com

Chile
ChileGlobal
Monjitas 392, Piso 15

Santiago, Chile
Molly Pollack -Directora ChileGlobal
+56 (2) 6389810
mpollack@imagendechile.cl

Colombia
Global Techbridge
10 South Third St, 3rd Floor
San Jose, CA 95113
Constanza Nieto - CEO
408-694-3683
constanza@globaltechbridge.com

Mexico
TechBA Silicon Valley
1737 N. First St. #110
San Jose, CA 95112
Jorge Zavala-CDO Chief Disruptive Officer
jorge.zavala@techba.com

Adolfo Tavera-CEO
adolfor.tavera@techba.com

Jose Mendez-Director, Call Center Program
jose.mendez@techba.com

Ana de la Vega, Office Manager
editor@techba.com

USA
Citrix Systems
Citrix Start Up Accelerator

4555 Great America Parkway
Santa Clara, CA 95054
John McIntyre - Senior Director
408-790-8227(T)
408-391-0404(M)
john.mcintyre@citrix.com

National Business Incubator Association
7027 E. Kenyon Dr.
Tucson, AZ 95054
Ana Grief-International Programs Officer
520-869-1775
agreif@nbia.org

US Market Access Center
Alfredo Coppola - CEO
408-351-3300
alfredo@usmarketaccess.com

Europe
Belgium
Flanders Investment and Trade
Consulate General of Belgium
155 Montgomery Street suite 204
San Francisco, CA 94104
Annik Bouquet-Director of Technology
415-546-5255(T)
415-546-3144(M)
annik.bouquet@fitaagency.com

Catalonia
Government of Catalonia, Ministry of Innovation, Universities and Entrepreneurial Affairs

10 South Third St, 3rd Floor
San Jose, CA 94113
Anselm Bossacoma - Executive Director
408-627-7226
anselm@copcalosangeles.com

Czech Republic
CzechInvest - East Coast
321 East 73rd St
New York, NY 10021
Jan Fried-Head of East Coast Operations
+1 347 216 93 55
jan.fried@czechinvest.com
CzechInvest - West Coast
440 N Wolfe Rd.
Sunnyvale, CA, 94085

Lenka Kucerova-Head of West Coast Operations
Office: 408 524 1690
Mobile: +1 415 794 0665
lenka.kucerova@czechinvest.org

Denmark
Innovation Center Denmark
200 Page Mill Road
Palo Alto, CA 94306
Camilla Rygaard-Hjalsted - Executive Director
crh@innovationcenterdenmark.com
www.innovationcenterdenmark.com
650 543 3181

Lene Sjorslev Schulze-Account Manager
650-543-3182(T)

415 812 6646 (M)
lsa@innovationcenterdenmark.com

Ms. Marianna Lubanski - Director of Innovation Center Denmark, Silicon Valley
mlu@innovationcenterdenmark.com
650 543 3180
Ministry of Foreign Affairs of Denmark
2, Asiatisk Plads, DK-1448
Copenhagen K, Denmark
Anita Nielsen-Investment Manager, Clean Tech
650-543-3186
anitni@um.dk

Estonia
Enterprise Estonia
440 N. Wolfe Rd.
Sunnyvale, CA 94085
Andrus Viirg - Director of Enterprise Estonia, Silicon Valley
415-335-3843
Andrus.Viirg@eas.ee
www.eas.ee

Finland
FinPro
3945 Freedom Circle, suite 110
Santa Clara, CA 95054
Pekka Pärnänen - Head of Finpro Silicon Valley
408-748-7400(T)
408-799-6655(M)
pekka.parnanen@finpro.fi
http://www.finpro.fi

Mika Eriksson-Director, Client Relations
mika.eriksson@finpro.fi

Tekes
3945 Freedom Circle, Suite 110
Santa Clara, CA 95054
Kaarlela Mirja - Head of Tekes Silicon Valley
408-748-7400(T)
408-893-8237(M)
mirja.kaarlela@tekes.fi
www.tekes.fi

Germany
GABA - German American Business Association
1715 Villa St, Ste G
Mountain View, CA 94041
Thomas Neubert
650-386-5015
chairman@gaba-network.org

PolyTechnos Venture-Partners
Promenadeplatz 12
D-80333 Munich
Germany
Dirk Kanngeiser
+49 (0) 89 2422 620
dirk.kanngeiser@polytechnos.com

Ireland
Enterprise Ireland
800 West El Camino Real, Suite 420
Mountain View, CA 94040

David Smith
650-294-4082
David.Smith@enterprise-ireland.com
http://americas.enterprise-ireland.com
Simone Boswell
SVP Digital Media, Internet, Entertainment
simone.boswell@enterprise-ireland.com

Irish Innovation Center News
189 W. Santa Clara Street
San Jose, CA 95113
John Stanton
President
408.380.7200
john.stanton@irishic.com

Estonia
Enterprise Estonia
440 N. Wolfe Rd.
Sunnyvale, CA 94085

Andrus Viirg
Director of Enterprise Estonia, Silicon Valley
415-335-3843
Andrus.Viirg@eas.ee

Italy
Business Association Italy America – BAIA
333 Market Street
25th Floor
San Francisco, California 94105

Marco Marinucci
650-253-7804
mmarinucci@gmail.com
mmarinucci.ixmba2005@alumno.ie.edu
http://www.baia-network.org/

Fabrizio Capobianco
fabricapo@gmail.com
http://www.linkedin.com/groups/
Mind-Bridge-Mentors-3825878

Norway
Innovation Norway
20 California St., 6th Floor
San Francisco, CA 94111
Anne Hovi Worsoe - Director
415-986-0765
anne.worsoe@innovationnorway.no

Ase Petterson Bailey
415-986-0765
ase.pettersen.bailey@innovationnorway.no
Royal Norwegian Counsel General
20 California St., 6th Floor
San Francisco, CA 94111

Sten Arne Rosnes - Counsel General
415-986-0766(T)
sten.arne.rosnes@mfa.no
Strategic Business Insights
333 Ravenswood Avenue
Menlo Park, CA 94025

Eilif Trondsen, Ph.D. - Program and Research Director
650-859-2665(T)
etrondsen@sbi-i.com
Http://www.strategicbusinessinsights.com
http://www.linkedin.com/in/eiliftrondsenvwc

Scotland
Scottish Development International
Calum Lancastle - Senior Vice President, U.S. Western Region
calum.lancastle@scotent.co.uk

Spain
Spain Nexus
145 Vallejo Street
San Francisco, USA
Jose Mateos
415-963-1180
josemateos@wikreate-expansion.com
http://www.spainnexus.com/

StepOne Ventures Silicon Valley
350 Townsend St. Suite 307
San Francisco, CA 94107
Beto Juarez
210-573-1112(M)
beto@stepone.com
www.stepone.com
www.linkedin.com/in/betojuareziii

StepOne Madrid
Cécile Baux
+34 653 229 589
info@stepone.com

www.stepone.com
The Spain-U.S. Chamber of Commerce
145 Vallejo St, Ste 3
San Francisco, CA 94111

Isabel Arcones
iarcones@gmail.com
http://www.linkedin.com/in/iarcones
22@Barcelona
Àvila 138, 3a planta
08018 Barcelona

Andreu Vea
landreu@gmail.com

Sweden
Bootstrap Labs
540 University Ave, Third Fl, Ste 300
Palo Alto, CA 94301
Nicolai Wadstrom - CEO
415 935 1469
nicolai.wadstrom@bootstraplabs.com

Switzerland
Swissnex
730 Montgomery Street
San Francisco, CA 94111
Birgit Coleman - Innovation and Partnerships
415-912-5901 x105
birgit.coleman@swissnexSanFrancisco.org
www.swissnexSanFrancisco.org
Gioia Deucher

415-912-5901
gioia.deucher@swissnexsanfrancisco.org

UK
Tanner Highlen
http://www.linkedin.com/profile/view?id=62713261
World Bank
1818 H St NW
Washington DC, 20433
Jean-Louis Racine
+1-202-473-1719
jracine1@worldbank.org
www.worldbank.org

Asia
Australia
ANZA Technology Network
226 Broderick St
San Francisco, CA 94117
Viki Forrest - CEO
415-309-7068
viki@anzatechnet.com
www.anzatechnet.com
TangibleFuture, Inc.
1801 Bush St, Suite 114
San Francisco, CA 94109
Richard Caro
rgcaro@tangiblefuture.com
http://www.tangiblefuture.com

India
The Indus Entrepreneurs - TIE
www.tiesv.org

Vish Mishra
CEO
vish@tie.org
Kiran Kini Malhotra - Executive Director, TiE Silicon Valley
408.567.0700 ext. 233
kiran@tie.org

Japan
Jetro
201 Third St
San Francisco, CA 94103
Manabu Saito - Director Business Development
415-392-2523(T)
manubu_saito@jetro.go.jp
Jane Chung - Director, Public Relations
415-392-2523(T)
jane_chung@jetro.go.jp

Korea
NIPA
3003 N. First St. STE342
San Jose, CA95134
H. Kyu Lim - Head NIPA Silicon Valley
408-232-5467(T)
408-455-8266(M)
hklim@nipa.kr
Kotra-Korea Trade Investment Promotion Agency
3003 N. 1st St
San Jose, CA 95134
Kyoung Moo Kwon -Director of IT Service Center
408 432-5002(T)
kyoungmoo@kotra.or.kr

Malaysia
Malaysia Industrial Development Authority
226 Airport Parkway, Ste 480
San Jose, CA 95110
Sohaimi Sharif - Director, MIDA
408-392-0617(T)
midasanjose@aol.com

Singapore
IDA Singapore
3 Twin Dolphin Dr, Ste. 150
Redwood City, CA 94065
Joachim Ng
650-593-1716(T)
Joachim.Ng@ida.gov.sg
Jasmine Leng
650-593-1716
jasmine.leng@ida.gov.sg

Taiwan
ITRI
2880 Zanker Road, Suite 109,
San Jose, CA 95134
Sean Wang
408-428-9988 x 12
seanwang@itri.com

Made in the USA
Columbia, SC
25 September 2019